Anything with Spirit

Anything with Spirit

isaiah a. hines

ISBN: 979-8-9915011-1-8
Library of Congress Control Number: 2024950301

Book design by Deborah Thomas
Edited by Lonely Christopher
Author photograph by Shayla Kerr-Munsie
Cover image by Life-Of-Pix from Pixabay

NEW YORK STATE OF OPPORTUNITY. | Council on the Arts This book is made possible, in part, by the New York State Council on the Arts with the support of the office of the Governor and the New York State Legislature.

Roof Books
are published by Segue Foundation
300 Bowery Fl 2
New York, NY 10012
seguefoundation.com & roofbooks.com

Distributed by Independent Publishers Group/IPGbook.com

To my family:

In gratitude for my voice

CONTENTS

BLACK COMPOSITIONAL THOUGHTS

DARKER CLARITIES

SICK SOULS

AFTER LIGHT

POMP AND GLARE

Anything with spirit can get broke.

—Jordan Peele, *Nope*

BLACK COMPOSITIONAL THOUGHTS

When I
die
I'm sure
I will have a
Big Funeral…
Curiosity
Seekers…
coming to see
if I
am really
Dead…
Or just
trying to make
Trouble…

—Mari. E. Evans, "The Rebel"

I am a stranger
learning to worship the strangers
around me

whoever you are
whoever I may become.

—June Jordan, "These Poems"

Afropolarity

We don't all remember the awkward child
we once were
Loved. Light
but not all right
fighting for something
that can't or will not be.

This has let me see
from right here in this
perpendicular moment.
My vantage and my whim

tell me what exactly i feel ashamed
of, beloved.
Don't i want to be able to look back on those memories
 fondly?
Don't i want to know myself freely and loudly and openly
 again?
If so, dig this:

i am an addict. So, what, i hurt somebody,
a person.
So, now what? Begin from my ruined heart.

As a poet, my starting point is often public language.
That which can be represented via the common lexicon.

But i do have a voice. Northerner, city-man
sitting sorrowful and the worst thing
i could possibly imagine

is that there is absolutely nothing
wrong with me.

i think the universe has not
yet made up its mind about
me. An incantation, for zero captures
changes me like discovery, or rot,

asking if i'm really scared. Yes—
open, nevertheless; shake, writhe, and furl.
i will not hand you half an open hand.
i do it anyway
i begin again.

i am reminded of you thinking now
of where, how to position
my bed in my new room
something i wouldn't have noticed otherwise
is that when your bed is in the middle of the room,
you can rise more easily from sleep without waking
your partner.

i forget, at times, how borderline
i am; orbiting paranoid and cincophrenic black poles
of frigid and fervid liminality; ever feeling
one's thirdness; the counter-hegemony
of an idiom of one's own.

And i am grateful for that
which i do not yet understand
and will not. That, too,

even this cockeyed refrain,
i love.

We cursed folk—
still confused and crazed but maybe
we don't need that uncrossing.
For Elegguá
is beyond good or evil.

Yes, i am crazy.
i rest with the rawest black
personalities and granddaddy's
most sacred musicians.

Why polar bears are black

After William Carlos Williams

They have black skin.
Symbolizing resilience, patience, and determination
needed to survive in a harsh climate.

Animating arctic intelligences.
Living in the polar imaginary:
not no man's land.

Far from empty
and actually
teeming with life, really.

Do i love you still?

i don't want this story. i want a love story.
But this is a love story.
Then a different kind of love story.
This is the only one i have.
Goddamn it.

All the sweet stuff but it still hurts now
it still feels so terribly nasty now—
do you have anything for that?
Anything, a spell, a tincture, a cocktail for my particular
whelm?
No? Well, i'll simply die, then.
Goodbye, God!

You tell me i can still write a new story. i can
still tell a different story. Can't unwrite
what has been written after the end
after it is all said and done.

But i can only manage to interest myself in writing the poem
where we are in love and writing through the
pain, regardless.

Racism, wicked and depraved, produces wicked and depraved people

Don't act shocked.
Clawing my way to clarity.
Consistent in my inconsistency.

The only thing i have is talking.
The only thing i can offer you.
This desperate notation.

Ruined language

The first time i knew i was null was in the spring of 2017. Made object. Rendered.

"Isaiah Hines is a nigger," it read, i think. i wouldn't know. i never saw it myself. i was told. Imagine it in red spray paint. They covered it up with a big blue tarp. My name rung through the intercom. i was lifted from my Environmental Science class. The event was relayed to me.

Already, i knew that words did more than represent. That was part of why. Why i did not speak, that day. i went home. i didn't cry. i told my mom what happened, and she cried.

The artist cried as he looked around me, searched the air for his expiation.

In me he did not find redemption. He could not make pure my lack of tone or absolve his desire for control. i was not there. i did not see his face. i knew what he wanted.

> uncovering one's own suffering
>
> recovering oneself from heartbreak
>
> and sometimes i think i did it purely to make trouble

i was told it could not be called a hate crime because the victim in the crime was not a person, but an artificial grass polyethylene—the property of my high school. And as a piece of property, it was entitled to no legal protections from racist violence.

In this unremarkable legal maneuver i landed null.
i ruined language.

Language is what we do best

We need to still all
be able to find
each other after the end.
How will we recognize ourselves?

When it all is over (said and done)

are we still talking about
language?
i make a mess of things
and we still talk about.

Mixed emotions

This is my American voice,
multiplicitous,
duplicitous,
profoundly complex,

low-tech,
highly regionalized,
mixed states of being,
profoundly mixed up.

i was my own path

What romanticism are we subject to today?
The categories are commercial.

i tell myself, i haven't met all the people i'm gonna love in this life yet (including myself).

i give myself permission to wonder and to wander, to become this document. Unconditionally.

Why should i think i am sane? What grounds me temporarily between poles is my capacity to hurt or love others. The horror of adding to an atmosphere already saturated with violence, the miasma.

Some of us are people who, when we are hurting, we want to make others hurt and bring other people up in our hurt so that we may not be so lonely in our pain. This curse is inherited. We fairskinned or light complexioned black people. We multiracial people. We mixed up people. i call it having a little evil in me. i do hesitate to say this since i worry how that could be interpreted to mean something other than my best effort toward theodicy.

i don't know much about the other type of people other than the fact that i'm not that and i could spend a lifetime trying to be like that and get like that and i still probably never would.

Like the experience of straining one's eyes to see in the dark, especially after just having looked at a bright screen.

Black cope

Blackness and stoicism don't mix
to me.

We must constantly
expose the plot
to make blackness consonant
with suffering.

Does blackness necessarily index suffering?
How could you be null without value judgment?

embarrassed by how much technology is still mystified for me
i'm ridden with guilt
for what i've done and shame
for what i haven't but may

you should be careful around me
making sure of avoiding
potential danger, mishap,
or harm; caution

i didn't realize that
i already had a definition

i didn't realize
i already had a name

be careful for what may contain
anger

be cautious of what may conceal
resentment

i do want to be a part of this world

And i'd like to tell you about this. i'd like to share this with you.

This is not a happy story. This is a story of grief. Of feeling
the in-between. This is about suicidal ideation, cruelty,
violence, abuse cycles, addiction, attachment, colonialism, race,
eroticism, fetishization,

strategically undefined
perhaps disordered identity
disordered personalities are still too stigmatizing

does anyone else have that evil in them?

My story is not new

i will not make another hurt because i am hurt
i will find truth within the cliches

catalyzing
becoming
alchemizing hopes and dissatisfactions
radicalizing; grasping at the root
turning our embodied/lived experiences into shareable wis-
doms; gnosis

making other hurt because you're hurt.

i am a metallurgic poet; i weld
like Viriato da Cruz is a telluric poet
a transdisciplinary materials scientist

us black Columbia dropouts—
Hurston, Hughes, Hill:
we a baaddd people

Being drawn

At times he is the only thing. At times he is everything: taking up all the space i forgot my self even existed as. At times i want nothing more than to be included, be part of the club. Grieving the life i thought i was supposed to, i could have had. If i hadn't been so black and queer and mad. If not for my afro-polarity. Could i have had what white people hope for? i want nothing more than to write a disgusting poem. To be a sick freak in the permanency of print with you looking on. And i'm the disgruntled ex. The scorned woman. Losing language. i wake myself out of my sleep to write and still. And my dog snores in the bed next to me. And i strain to see my lost thoughts now on the other side of a dark room.

This dependence is its own kind of elitism

i need to learn to be more self-sufficient. In doing so i will realize how i am not just *my* self but a self-constituted by many; a self comprised of many people's contributions; so that
i am simultaneously my own but not all my own.

i hate routines, or i am bad at sticking to routines.
The only thing i ever seem to do routinely is drugs.
Regular
Consistent
The only things i have ever done consistently are drugs.

Scared my clamor of emotion indicates neurosis or sociopathy.

Divine timing

Occasional, unofficial sojourns with reality. Where i live is not reality. i live in the null space. A liminal maneuver of creation. this is where i dwell. i'm his is where i live. In the null spacetime. Blackqueer spatiotemporal zone of indeterminacy

Elaborate: to make a laboratory out of you.

Polar night

i don't understand i won't understand
Something i'm doing to myself
My fear is that somewhere the suffering feels good
i don't want to let go
i refuse to let go
There's no chance i'll let go.
To what i wanted and feel that i even had, if only for a moment
Torturing myself
i let go.

Poem

Orbiting poles of shame and guilt
making circuits it still knock
me over n leave me breathless
cross. spiral. whirl.

A long walk

What are we talking toward?
We must continuously reorient ourselves toward liberation.
Asking the questions that will help
Us get free.

DARKER CLARITIES

Sky thief

A shadow fell to the ground behind me.
I ran but the shadow followed
until it ate up the whole world around me.
I looked up at the sky and gasped.
It has turned black as midnight,
as if the sun had gone
out. I was bathed in the black
of the sky. I knew I was being watched by
unseen eyes. I was petrified.
I screamed for help but no sound
came out. Then finally I found
my voice. I yelled,
"Stop! Let the light shine freely!"
And it did,
I can make a difference.
Now I believe, the sun
shone brightly through the
darkness. My fear was replaced
by joy. I laughed out loud.
The sun came back.
Finally it was over.
But sometimes I still wonder
who stole it—the sky I mean.

—isaiah a. hines, age 11
"Sky thief," *The Burlington Free Press*

Spitfire

i swallow it all
leaving
not even a drop
left of love
or despite
real, undeniable pain
i drink it all
up, writhing
because it blisters
as it goes down
there is nothing
more but my love
which was grief
persisting, and
eating up
my voice which
choked on desperate
wanting and
peering at death.

Atlantic meridional overturning circulation collapse

While the world
and you grow cold,
i glare,
incandescent with agony,
becoming brighter
by this same metaphysic.
i cracked
open my exterior
for you, ate your aura
but you dis-
placed
my center, my end.
That becomes the reason
for our earlier trials
growing to light.

Torn apart by circumstance,
this is not my fantasy.

Let me tell you how to meet the day

After Mari Evans

There really are no bad poems, are there?
Like people, there are poems
that you write
that you distrust, poems
which you have to write
in order to write the poems you want
to write; and to be the poet you want
to be, these poems that aren't quite good enough and could be
better and are not the
best, to you.
You write the poem
anyway, knowing somewhere
in you it won't be the last.
That is how
you meet the day,
understanding this will be
the reason you are still a writer,
years later, still a poet—
because of this here poem
that you be.

If i was braver

i'd hold his hand
the first time
and feed him:
unafraid and proud.

If i was braver
i'd sing hello
Ms. Giovanni,
i think you're grand.

If i was braver
i'd scream
"Free Palestine! Free Sudan! Free Congo!"
before uttering a word.

When i do, i can
and when i can't,
i do it anyway.
Not brave, just reckless.

We are all variations on a theme

For Reuben

We travel much farther
cover much greater distances
to still end up sidereal
in someone else's backyard.
We go all the way to the pole
and choose the equator.
Polarity is also a quality of light:
how we refract
what would otherwise be just
experience; living criteria
that returns changed
in profound difference and
rebellious circuitry

Poem

i want to make sense of things with you
i want senseless moments with you
i want to make nothing with you
curious to the point of self-immolation

Der niemandslicht

After Paul Celan

i wish to be no one's light.
We are
never knowing a thing
in its entirety.

i wish to be the light of no one:
illuminating no one's heart
—that which is home to no
transparent beasts.

A penumbra, at rate.
A murk, marked safe
An out
from the open

: free of anything that
makes clear

Bridging the me and the you

After Margaret Walker

In order for me to feel
content, complete speaking
in plurals, asking
"who are we?"
i first must make myself
accountable, catalogued
and categorized
unless there were something
like you,
like love
to take me
to see the sunrise
on a mountaintop,
where i remark quietly,
"A union of the two worlds must be,"
and you respond,
"You mean the world to me."
Suddenly we are
of the same world.

It's time

Now i re-narrate my own story.
i will no longer allow my story to be told by others.
i will not allow myself to by painted by anyone who
  does not love me.
i'll be the thorn in your side.
i'd like to talk about a painting.

The thing that makes you combative
  requires gentleness only.
Not everyone has caused as much harm in the world as i have.
Why do those who can make so much good also spread so much
  pain:
i'll be your fancy clown
gesticulating this operation
  of healing for the both of us

SICK SOULS

Rabbit brain

my mind is like a rabbit
it bounces all around
it has become a habit
all of a sudden i hear the sound

of my mind jumping like a rabbit
i get new ideas in a snap
when my mind hops like a rabbit
new thoughts fill an empty gap"

—isaiah a. hines, age 12
"Rabbit brain," *The Magic Book of Poems*

This shouldn't be so hard. This is part of the continuum. And we do go on. Scared. Unsure. Troubled by the dark. Blinded by desire. We do go on. We continue. And because it isn't perfect. Because it is hard. Someone will see that someone tried. And someone will know that someone loves.

—Nikki Giovanni, "Today: For Mari Evans"

Unfinished business

Those of us who
deal in doubt

Those who are wrestling
with writing about family
genealogies, little histories

Maybe
we are our parents'
unfinished business

The residue of
ancestors'
deferred dreams, and ours

We who are hurt in love
we who speak from a place
of pain

We who have failed to contribute
knowledge and information
deemed necessary

For a better world
and an understanding of
the human experience within it

Let me speak.
Take me serious.
Humor me.

Return the gesture.

Let me begin

From my dissatisfactions
and hopes, the point of
my inability to provide

An objective perspective,
my commitment to reducing
suffering wherever it arises,

Whether self-inflicted
or not. The disappointment
of my subjectivity

This account is interested

i do have an agenda i do
this to get free and
get all my peoples free

My community
we who have lost faith
and founded truths

Previously unknown to
man, we welded,
built cathedrals

Weathered every storm
we who have fallen from grace
with each blow,

i send out a new root
with each fall,
i earn the soil's trust i become

Born, live, or die. Steady, we already
have everything we need.
i already have everything

i need to be.
They say nobody could

Have known.
They say it was unforeseeable
but some did know.

How did they know what they knew?
Are we to think it is mere coincidence?
Even as we generate evidence

That suggests the possibility

Poem

Ever feeling that i care too much to be in this world.
Soon, surely i'll be torn asunder
as DuBois said.
Any day now.

Wrist icy

Small enough it could be blamed on anything and
small enough that it still elicited
the kind of cut i wanted
or my fear wanted
to be felt more fully, but who
can be sure? Even these scars

can be unsure.

Grow my genealogy

Neither brave nor purely
shameful; neither anything worth
repeating nor actual terror;

neither i nor you will
ever fully claim it;
was it a virtual racial terror?

A psychodrama,
just ordinary.

Tonight

The best things happen when you are truthful with yourself
and others.

Like studies of contact,
there are multiple processes involved
unseen; cold sweat.

It can be hard
to find your voice amongst the voices.

A poem written between two sleeps and
no wake.

An apophenic notebook

is something that you would use
to register patterns that you notice
and in doing so you'd also be-
come, experience apophenia.

Poem

Is racial consciousness just a means
of escaping control of white masters?
What are dangers (and possibilities)
of seeing it as more or less than this?

Politics of the periphery

Piece of wind.
Peace of mind.
Politics of self-
description.

i see it as a strange
and depoliticized place,
evacuated of meaning
yet symbolically full.

Being (un)noticeable

Diagressions

Avulsion:
abandon paths that no longer serve you, there is no supposed to be.

Digress:
turn aside especially from the main
subject of attention or course of argument.

Aggression:
forceful action or procedure especially
when intended to dominate or master
the practice of making attacks or encroachments
hostile, injurious, or destructive
behavior or outlook
especially when caused by frustration.
Understanding how masculinity wears me, at times.

Egress:
the place or means of going out;
the action or right of going or coming out;
to go or come out.

A postcolonial, postdiscipline love story

And heartbreak but that is a given, undeniable.
Inevitably it hurts
more than it matters.
It does not seem to matter

the level or degree of certainty
i think that i feel that i **know**.
This cannot be all that there is.
Fuck your fundamental opposition.

i demand a life and a world
in which we need not suffer
to the degree and extent
to which we do today

i do not know
if there is a life without
suffering. If there is,
we do not, cannot know it.

Desires so strong and
impracticable it hurts.
Love can hardly be described
as a logical or reasonable force.

Teaching myself to fall
out of love with him may be
as im/possible and improbable
as learning to recover from postcolonial heartbreak

Proprioception

Like how a deer is incredibly aware
of its antlers,
able to navigate them with such precision,
an extension of their body.

Hmm, i'm fucked up? Nah, i'm not. Nigga i'm fuckin REAL

There is a fundamental incompatibility between human and computer patterns of thinking or processing information.

i am interested in all the ways that we work to resolve this existential problem, to resolve the paradox, resolve the manifold

i have a suspicion that the increasing technologization of society has much to do with this… but it is not the end. null is not the end. Null is not dead.

Null means ask questions.

AFTER LIGHT

As a singer grows older
His conception goes a little deeper
Because he lives life and
He understands what he's trying to say a little more
As the singer tries to find out what's happening in life
It gives him a better insight
On telling the story of the song he's trying to sing.

—Sam Cooke's Radio Interview,
audio sampled in "Dayglo Reflection,"
XL Recording

In the oldest black man's court
With its lawyers and judges and money and men
Sits our northern Isaiah in the City of New York.
There the sorrow of the prophet
Marks his word and his action and his thought
Sorrow sits upon his saddened face and declares his destiny.

—Margaret Walker, "Isaiah"

A stone's throw, in a crystal world

Growing harder,
more sensitive,
what says soft but could not mean?
Cracks
in the glass.
No,
a fiver,
tucked.
Distance or duration?
Or depth
of noticing.
Iotas seen,
this is what you should know.
All that you need.

The wordwork

Bridge for sale.
It don't matter if the devil give credit.
Somebody has got to give it.
Doubly struck: encruzilhada.

Mystics of modern mechanics:
the quantum computer. In times like this,
the workings of the enchantment
become most palpable and visible.

i loved my friend

Because of the side of the
equation on which i have fallen,
i can see a perspective
that is explosive possibility.

An equation toward a scalar literacy

What could i mean?
Is what i mean what i be?
What else could i be, or mean?
What do you and i, here, mean?
We get to do this together
We get to make this together, right.
i am strategic, and political.
We get to decide; choose
What we should mean, here
Now,
After light.

How to operate an equator

Buy ink for printer.
Know when to quit.
How to persist in a mindstorm.
Be glass (half wanting or half filled).
How to read entrails.
Learn how to operate a printer.
Nourish your unfed body.
Attend.
Sweat it out.
Know how to be along for the ride.
Never stop talking about how great it is to be black cause i ain't gotta do shit but stay black and die translated and a maricón, a pussy boy.

The only thing i have to do
is mantener surrender to
reading black and being red.
El ánimo elevado.
Be PLEASING.
Know where your holes are
DON'T DO THIS is all i get to do:
train, narrowing. Never stop.

As [art] object ground.
Everything's sounds.
The wind's ontology.
Its ensemble.
Knowing how to ride
simultaneities;
waves.

How to slow optics;
pilot waves;
astral planes.
Hum.
Live in visual climates by which you become
sound,
wind,
rain, and fog.
Touch the surface of the breath
or go unfilled again.

Collect
Collapse
The fruit
The fig
The encounter
Fibrous ellipsoid of time
Have something to give in return this time
Take comfort in crossing unfathomable and precise distances to
Celebrate every tiny ceremonies.
Return.
Know when to return from wanting to be everything.

How to find how.
Where islands are a mechanism for knowing
how to sense your own internal level of ink.
Remote at/tunings.
Blacknesses.
Control.
Live in un un-integrated circuit chip.
How to be light emitted though a prism at the bottom of a
well;

No hay ley para la información.
How to outperform an immortal jinx.
Fire
Language
Clay
Geometries of the liver.
How to remember when you were a noise spinning inside all things.

Black don't crack

> I sell the shadow to support the substance
> —Sojourner Truth

The library is that
which makes communication possible.
So what is the source of
our ill-literacies?
This library is postmodern
and neocolonial.
So why should we expect it
to love us the way
we love each other or

we love our children.
Where is the public?
My public is at the library.
My library is black.
And i can walk into it
barefoot
and feel at home.

Can an array of accounts,
when taken together,
constitute a new kind
of account? Despite the radical
imbalance in representations.
A sum, gets treated as
a single entity.

What else but love

could i feel when i see
our bronze intermolding, forever
enduring in grace,
an intricate quilt or
defiant tapestry
tones that sound nothing
but harmonious to me.
The most good looking
and holy music.

Love editing :: love writing

i thought we were the same kind of artist.
i'm trying to come to terms with what Reuben
and Demian said
about the writing world (and the art world)
requiring some sacrifice,
this violence of making it, being made
in this wearily, jadedly laced world.
Am i happy?
What have i done with the time?
All i have done is assume
the position of stars
in the sky of polar nights:
almost frozen
in place but periodically,
dependably growing bright.
i've had to make
so many journeys
to the most remote places and
i still collapse
under your weight,
as if you were your own
gravitational attraction.

Alma mater

i burned
my ticket to class mobility;
jumped out of the moving vehicle of success
as defined by secular humanism;
leapt from the plane that would've carried me to Paris.
Touched by whiteness and left
damaged.
Touched by lightness and left
damaged.
Touched by the elite and wrote,
wounded.
i touched language's
escape and left
ruined.

Small data

Black at and as the origin
Techne, cargo and tools
Constructors

Whiteness demands
Something closer to demolition or development
White extracts every pixel that makes up your smile

According to the very nature of things
Obligation is precisely that which you can reject
Or else it would be a matter of fact

A matter of responding to stress
An unreceptiveness to unresponsiveness
A command chain rolling over, unbothered

The uses of informatics, agreements of
Wanting vaguely to be nothing more than included the part
Of things, of labors, to be died of assumption, distributed

Of giants, unless the DIY citizens
Can consume the needs. There is no press
That performs this imperial function

That will respond to requests for further clarification. No keys.
Disasters. Economic recession. Chronic pain with no source.
War. Greater racism and environmental degradation

All of this is simply according to the nature of things
This is not my fantasy
This is how it seems to be that it works

Join the mumble club
Grounded in critical race babble, foraging and dis-
Figuring, farming documents of
Small data

Poem

If you get me in a room,
i will perform like any
caged animal; strained,

stumbling after a lost
thought. Eating
crumbs off the floor.

Poetic controversy

After Amiri Baraka

My work is difficult, intricate,
layered—not unlike my self.
i am not a disagreeable person.

i am most unforgettable.
See how i talk past my self
and you, read past me,

finding only your self,
already busy, meeting
in the room made by

your head.
Line by line,
thread by thread,

who will be the last
letter standing? Thrust
forth through iron, snow, and dread.

Enchantment

break the spell
fuck what you wanted
break the curse
fuck what's been handed to you
break the cycle
fuck this now and put down that weight
you've carried
so strong, so blue
for so long
don't wait a another moment
before casting
yourself a way of riding the wake,
birth a palm, sticking out
from a floating stone
and land,
rest for a while
in the tardiness.
The boat
is breaking away
leaving you on the shore
not alone, but
lonely in your new world.
Will this gap,
so strong, so blue
break you past the elastic
or set you flowin'
i'll take you
sinners to heaven
and hell on earth,
so strong, so blue.

the bed beneath my nails

i love it when
my fingernails
already, are grown:
changed by
my distracted mouth,
gazing at a miracle—his
hands.
It's okay that we lose sight of each other sometimes,
as long as we know how to find our way back together.
The distribution of weights
the distribution of waits
the distributions of griefs
    is vastly uneven
how emotions
    are distributed across
    our populations.

Surveyor's waltz no. 1

Today i weld a new language for our story, so intricate and opaque, we have been to each other and ourselves.

Not creating something out of nothing for there was much that came before, that primed and prepared us for this. The metals. The earth in the soil. Souls alloyed with iron blacker than carbon.

This myth is my mourning and my expiation. Making me
is metallurgic, almost alchemical, unverifiable and divine,
a precise metamorphosis of a different kind.

You made a world in me.

Let me weave a lace of truths strong enough, harplike in sound and form as the lace of steel that wings the Verrazzano bridge.

Is there no victim or no one to hold responsible? No one to witness the carnage? A victim of no one in particular other than empire and racial capitalism and the ways they permeate a space, seeping in and making themselves felt in our quiet lives and most mundane moments.

Accountable to no one, the violence is Supreme, pristine.
You feel frigid now because i am close to the equator now and now you grow extreme. i appear only in increments, no show, no scene, nothing left worth looking at. Slow, strange, and menacing.

Why do you always turn away from me.

Working the miracle

By miracle i came to you
landed on your shores
valued instantly
and incrementally became nil.

God in this grief
i have become born
a viviparous life, die or be
sent out to a new estuary.

Constantly searching
for something like equilibrium
that i will never get for
more than a moment.

POMP AND GLARE

Across up in the sky
But everybody wanna ask me why
What good do your words do
if they can't understand you?

—Erykah Badu, "…& On"

Anyone who writes is a seeker. You look at a blank page and you're seeking. The role is assigned to us and never removed. I think this is an unbelievable blessing.

—Louise Glück interviewed by Henri Cole, 2021

Rock my soul

How much stress i can withstand
How much strain my body can take
That biker snuck up on me
Yellow downers, purple flowers
What is the bird call that i have heard all these years?
To whom does this voice belong?
The bottom of my hands hurt from falling in the bowl.
i was so brave today. Now i'm not.

Saludo a elegguá

The door is open.
i am son and child and follower.
i walk with him at night.
He tricks me,
tucks me
in the
corner.

Nightbring

that's that deep deep deep knowing feeling
deep
deeper than you could ever reach
deeper than you could ever dig
it will remain unearthed
it is not finished
the knowing is unfinished
my living is not complete

i keep this for me i hold on to this for me and i
must, must like i must breathe i
must hold on tight.

the continuum of meaning wherein truth lies
what they've said warped with their white ways
is not the truth
not the singularity
i know. now.

we don't own it
we don't have it
i wouldn't be so naïve as to think that i hold it
but i hold on to grasp at the search for the
truths
that lie
dark

My new york poem

is where i had my best
and my brightest moments
my darkest and my
lightest moments of hope
floating moments of no hope
places of nope—hopelessness
places of documentary
that was my poetics
my whelm and where my
sweetest moments are buried
inured to the violence
discipline sounds so foreign
a language i could never
learn to speak
where i lost my innocence
again and again and
made a mess of things all
over again and again and
again i board the train
swearing i'm not hoping
to run into you
my immense fear
immense architectures
unthinkable infrastructures, feats
of nature and brilliance
in the information we make
with our bodies that hum
we make we drum

Lua nha testemunha

Progress without redemption
spinning into danger
spinning into threat
spinning into liability
spinning and not safe
spin not to be engaged
spine untouchable
spinning more trouble than it's worth
and i understood
and redeemed myself
condemning your cold
front and steelo
that i didn't think
was in your nature.

Picking up where i left off

i am myth,
not man
not legend.
i don't dictate

which way
is upright
or orient
any humans.

i am myth,
not map
not finished.
i grow less

gaunt; remade
in grace, and
more precise
less knowable.

Pomp and glare

And what if you're the protagonist in my story, too?
You drive the plot.
How do you do what you do?
Already a nothing
In you i remembered my worst
Became anything i had
Agreed to be by birth
i speak with sureness but
Had i forgot which side of the equation
i fall on?
Had i thought i could change fate
Or control truth?
The only thing left to do is choose
Quiet as it's kept
Niggas is gay, too.

Why don't we dance more?

It leaves me breathless
knocks the wind
out of me, every time.
How much
i don't know
how much
i have lost and forgotten
so much.
My afroinsularity
my provincialisms
stunt me
and i take pleasure
in an empty gap.

Poem

For Manuel

That's all
i am asking for:
someone to return
the gesture.

Surveyor's waltz no. 2

Are not the brightest stars
the coldest?
i'm sabotaging myself because i'm
terrified to be seen

because visibility could mean my end.
Scared people will recoil
from me once they know.
If being visible could mean my doom

how will i ever be seen?

i wish to know, I think
that i know.
i'm so tired
of carrying it.

But i do not know what it means
to put it down.
It is so telling when people respond,
"I can't believe you're treating me like a nigger."

Protocol & punishment

Can't you understand
that i can't just do
what you do?
i'll spend my whole life

gesturing toward it—
performing this calculation—
and it still can't, or will not,
be.

i have had to become
literate; weld
so many new languages
for such unwieldy grief.

the best in language since 1976

Recent & Selected Titles

- WINDOWS 85 by Chris Campanioni, 160 pp. $20
- BUMBLEBEES by Deborah Meadows, 100 pp. $20
- THROUGH A WINDOW by Norman Fischer, 104 pp. $20
- SECRET SOUNDS OF PONDS by David Rothenberg, 138 pp. $29.95
- HAND ME THE LIMITS by Ted Rees, 130 pp. $20
- TGIRL.JPG by Sol Cabrini, 138 pp. $29.95
- THE POLITICS OF HOPE (After the War): Selected and New Poems by Dubravka Djuric, Biljana D. Obradovic (translator), 248 pp. $25
- BAINBRIDGE ISLAND NOTEBOOK by Uche Nduka, 148 pp. $20
- MAMMAL by Richard Loranger, 128 pp. $20
- EXCURSIVE by Elizabeth Robinson, 140 pp. $20
- I, BOOMBOX by Robert Glück, 194 pp. $20
- FOR TRAPPED THINGS by Brian Kim Stefans, 138 pp. $20
- TRUE ACCOUNT OF TALKING TO THE 7 IN SUNNYSIDE by Paolo Javier, 192 pp. $20
- THE NIGHT BEFORE THE DAY ON WHICH by Jean Day, 118 pp. $20
- MINE ECLOGUE by Jacob Kahn, 104 pp. $20
- SCISSORWORK by Uche Nduka, 150 pp. $20
- THIEF OF HEARTS by Maxwell Owen Clark, 116 pp. $20
- DOG DAY ECONOMY by Ted Rees, 138 pp. $20
- THE NERVE EPISTLE by Sarah Riggs, 110 pp. $20
- QUANUNDRUM: [i will be your many angled thing] by Edwin Torres, 128 pp. $20
- FETAL POSITION by Holly Melgard, 110 pp. $20
- DEATH & DISASTER SERIES by Lonely Christopher, 192 pp. $20
- THE COMBUSTION CYCLE by Will Alexander, 614 pp. $25

Roof Books are published by
Segue Foundation / seguefoundation.com
and distributed by Roof Books / roofbooks.com &
Independent Publishers Group / IPGbook.com